FINDING PURPOSE IN THE DARKNESS

A MOTHER'S JOURNEY THROUGH CHILD LOSS

CRYSTAL FOSTER

Thank you for all the support & the kind words.
♡ Crystal

Printed in the United States of America

First Printing Edition, 2024

ISBN 978-1-964165-17-2

Dedication

To my beloved son AJ,

I loved you for your whole life, and I will miss you for the rest of mine. Your absence has left a void that nothing can fill, but your memory remains a guiding light in my darkest moments. Your laughter, kindness, and beautiful spirit will forever be etched in my heart.

"Wherever a beautiful soul has been, there is a trail of beautiful memories."

Your beautiful soul left behind an unforgettable trail of love, joy, and precious memories. Though you are no longer here with me, the essence of who you were continues to inspire and uplift me every day.

Until we meet again, Meatball, you will always be the brightest star in my sky.

With all my love,

Mama

Acknowledgments

To my husband, Tim, thank you for staying by my side and being my #1 fan. I couldn't do this life without you.

To my boys Gavin & Keegan, I hope you know how much I love you. You boys are the light of my life, and I will always be your #1 fan.

To my family, friends, and coworkers, thank you for all of your support along the way and for picking me up on those bad days.

To my scholarship committee, I cannot say thank you enough. The scholarship and the foundation-n wouldn't be possible without y'alls help.

Author's Note

Crystal, married to her best friend Tim for 18 years, is a devoted mother, wife, nurse, and mental health advocate. AJ, her beloved middle son, holds a special place in her heart, even though he's no longer with her physically. In the past four years, Crystal has navigated the depths of grief while searching for her purpose in life and learning to live with a shattered heart.

Despite the pain of loss, Crystal finds solace in creating precious memories with her two other boys, Gavin and Keegan, alongside Tim. Whether it's exploring the beach, hiking through nature, or camping under the stars, she cherishes every moment spent with her family.

Professionally, Crystal's compassionate nature extends beyond her role as a nurse; she's also a dedicated mental health advocate, passionate about raising awareness and supporting those struggling with mental health challenges.

Through her journey of grief, love, and resilience, Crystal continues to inspire others with her strength and unwavering commitment to honoring AJ's memory while embracing the beauty of life's moments.

Table of Contents

Foreword

Dear Newly Bereaved Mother,

From one grieving mother's heart to another, I give you my deepest love and boundless strength during this immeasurably difficult time. There are no guidelines for navigating grief, and time seems to lose meaning after such a profound loss. I won't sugarcoat it for you. The pain you feel, the pain of losing your beloved son or daughter, will never go away completely. It will never be "okay" and life will never be the same. However, I can assure you that this will change. You adapt to carry this weight, to weave a life around the sadness and emptiness that surrounds you now. The pain lessens, and although it's never really gone, it becomes more tolerable over time. If you refuse to give in to despair, if you hold on to hope, you will find life again, albeit in a different tone. Colors may never return to their former vibrancy, but at some point they will flow back into your world. Time is not your ally, but rather your mentor, teaching you determination and strength. Listen to your heart above all else. Only you know what you need in this raw moment. Just breathe and do whatever you can to bring yourself into the next moment. There is no pressure to do more. It's about survival, one breath at a time, one moment at a time. There is no timetable for grief, no right or wrong way to navigate it. And despite the doubts you may have, know that you are not alone. Many of us are walking this path before you and many more will follow in your footsteps. When you are ready, contact those who are waiting for you. May they lift you up when you stumble, for they are filled with the strength born of a million broken hearts, united in time and space by the sadness that separates us from the rest of the world.

And if you persevere and hold on to your child's memory, one day you will find yourself reaching another grieving parent behind you. You will find that you too have the power to guide them on this difficult journey. But today and tomorrow as much as your heart dictates, just breathe and mourn, my sister. Breathe and grieve your child.And do it in a way that feels right to you. Just remember to breathe.

With unwavering solidarity and heartfelt compassion,

Crystal

CHAPTER ONE
Life Before the Nightmare

When tragedy strikes, time seems to freeze in the moment. For what seems like an eternity, we struggle to come to terms with unfortunate circumstances. An indefinite fissure appears in the fabric of events between a peaceful reality and the beginning of a nightmare. This disbelief leads to a million what-ifs – to regrets that keep you up at night. *What if I had done things differently? How did things go so wrong? If only I could turn back time...* These plaguing questions start to define every waking moment. A tragedy creates dissonance, and it's impossible to resolve this conflict until we accept the nightmare as a part of our harsh reality.

When my nightmare began, it turned my world upside-down. Nothing could have prepared me for it. That's not a hyperbolic statement; my world, indeed, was akin to a sweet dream. That's not to say I didn't endure my fair share of struggles. Just like everyone else, my family had conflicts. Sometimes, we struggled financially, we argued, and we faced problems. However, we always managed to persevere through those circumstances as a close-knit family.

Before the despair of a dark night, there is always the bliss of a bright day. My joyful days began quite early on in life when I fell in love with Tim at age 20. I met the love of my life when I was only in middle school. Back then, our different social circles kept us apart. I found him weird, and he thought I was stuck up. It wasn't until after graduation, through a mutual friend, that our paths crossed again. Hanging out as a group, something sparked. Young and silly at 19 and 20, we were having the time of our lives. Initially, we tried to keep our relationship a secret. However, we were inseparable, and within months, we were officially in a relationship.

By October 2002, he'd moved in with me at my parents' place. We were head over heels, spending every waking moment together. People criticized us. "It wouldn't last," we were told, but we brushed them off, living in our own loved-up bubble.

When September 2003 rolled around, we were in for a huge surprise! I was pregnant! We were both young, so I was naturally quite scared. Both of us were unsure of this parenthood thing. However, I did what every young mother does; I devoured books, did all the research, and decided to embrace my unborn child. With my mom by my side, I felt like we could handle it. Tim's parents were close, too, and they all formed a strong support system.

Come June 2004, Gavin Taylor was born. He was a perfect nine-pound bundle of joy. When I held him in my arms, I realized I never knew I could love someone so fiercely. My baby boy was an angel. He had a perfect temperament, slept through the night, and he was a growing ball of sunshine.

We weren't the parents who sought babysitters. We took our son everywhere, no matter the occasion. Whether we were headed to the friends' parties or dinners out, the boys were part of the fun. As we were still living with my parents, everything was manageable. Gavin thrived on our laid-back approach as well. We didn't have any rigid schedules or rules in place. We wanted to cherish every moment together and watch our firstborn bloom with wide-eyed wonder.

After having Gavin, we decided to transition from restaurant work. Tim started a new, more stable job at a metal recycling plant in late 2004. Meanwhile, in January 2005, I embarked on my journey to become a nurse. The early months of nursing school were a juggling act. I managed to stay home with Gavin, attending classes while Tim shouldered the bills. By mid-2005, I started waitressing for extra income.

We weren't keen on staying at my parent's house forever. Therefore, we started saving diligently, dreaming of our future as a little family. By early 2008, I graduated nursing school, and soon after, we took the plunge, and moved out on our own. We found a place near both of our parents' places to ensure that their support stayed close.

My first nursing job brought a whirlwind of changes - a young child, a new career, a new home, and the anxieties that came with them. However, Tim and I took it in stride.

Just when we started feeling like we had a handle on things, fate took us by surprise again. I was pregnant with another boy! Baby number two, Aidan Joseph, joined us in May 2009. Unlike Gavin's smooth pregnancy, Aidan kept me on edge. My little boy was eager to arrive early, and he triggered multiple false labor scares before finally gracing us with his eight-pound, ten-ounce presence at 38 weeks.

AJ was a ball of infectious joy. Even as an infant, he was full of life. He could melt hearts with his smile and contagious giggles. When his big brother, would be outside playing, AJ would follow Gavin around. Although he was just a few years old, his curiosity knew no bounds. He would dig in the dirt, find little bugs, and tote them around like they were his friends.

With the addition of a mischievous little family member, our responsibilities grew. We required someone to look after the kids. Around that time, my mom's health issues forced her to retire. Luckily, she came to our rescue again! Who wouldn't love having grandma doting on their kids? Every morning, she'd be at our doorstep before dawn, whisking the boys away while I went on my long commutes and demanding shifts.

In 2012, when my parent's financial struggles became apparent, we made a joint decision. Moving back in with my parents benefited everyone. Tim and I helped with the bills, while my parents became built-in babysitters, readily available without the daily commute. It was chaotic, that's for sure. After all, we were a rowdy, bustling extended family under one roof. However, the boys thrived in that carefree environment. Moreover, my cousin lived nearby, too, and her kids added to the fun within the ever-growing circle.

My parents lived on an old farm. Our property was vast, with barns and fields stretching as far as the eye could see. We were always outdoors, exploring and embarking on adventures within our expansive domain. As my kids grew, there were still a couple of fields located across the street from us. Between those fields, there was a charming irrigation ditch that ran through the field. One section of the ditch always held water, drawing the kids in like a magnet. They spent hours searching for frogs, turtles, and any other critters they could find. Those were truly magical times, filled with laughter and the joy of discovery.

AJ quickly grew fond of this place as one of his favorite spots to play, fully embracing his adventurous, boyish nature with a love for dirt, mud, and all kinds of creatures. During this time, Gavin was around seven or eight years old, while AJ was about two or three years old. The boys were equally as involved in sports. Gavin started playing soccer at age five, while AJ, despite being too young to actively participate, would eagerly cheer his brother on from the sidelines, always keen to join him on the field. Gavin was part of a soccer team named the Piranhas. That's how AJ's nickname came about. We affectionately called him "baby piranha" due to his constant presence and desire to play alongside the older kids.

Basketball, baseball, you name it, we were a family on the go. Whenever we found ourselves bored, we would either engage in board games or outdoor adventures. Apparently, this thrill for life ran in the family. Tim shared his sons' excitement and readily joined in, leading the boys on a dirt bike and four-wheeler escapades. They were practically riding before they could walk.

Our family was perfect. There wasn't much I would have wanted changed. However, when I heard about my pregnancy again, it filled my heart with immense joy. In early 2014, baby number three was on the way!

Living with my parents in their three-bedroom house, the thought of seven of us crammed together seemed infeasible. Luckily, my grandparents' old house next door had been vacant since their passing. My family was planning to sell it. Tim and I decided to buy the house. That gave us our own space and also kept the house in the family.

In October 2014, Keegan, another eight-pound, six-ounce bundle of joy, joined our family. While I adored him with all my heart, his personality was rather unique. Gavin, our eldest, was laid-back and easygoing, while AJ brimmed with curiosity and a thirst for exploration. However, Keegan quickly established himself as the "mean little brother."

From a very young age, he reveled in causing harmless mayhem. While his brothers would be innocently doing homework or playing, they would become unsuspecting victims of Keegan's "nibbling" attacks. He would bite their toes, backs, and anything within reach.

Balancing motherhood with my demanding nursing job, which involved three twelve-hour shifts a week, was a challenge. Life took another turn in mid-2015 when Tim's metal recycling plant shut down, leaving him unemployed. For a few months, he held down the fort at home while I juggled my schedule, transitioning from a full-time staff nurse to a local travel nurse, filling in wherever I was needed. Thankfully, Tim found a new job relatively quickly, joining my brother-in-law's family business, where he's happily thrived ever since.

With our careers secure and our own home, everything was going perfectly. Raising three boys, each with their distinct personalities, kept life interesting, to say the least. In eighth grade, Gavin's interests shifted from the sports field to the music room. He joined the marching band, dedicating himself to the sounds instead of the scores. On the other hand, AJ remained a sports enthusiast. Even when we weren't cheering on the sidelines, our home was a hub of activity.

As the boys grew, our three-bedroom house started feeling cramped. Despite having their own rooms in our bigger house, Gavin and AJ often preferred to share a space. They were simply that close. So, when we moved into our current three-bedroom home, they shared again while Keegan had his own room. But even that space wasn't enough for long.

There was an empty lot on the other side of my parents' house, so we decided to build our house there. In 2018, we moved in, and the house became our permanent residence.

Life continued its usual rhythm of sports, adventures, and laughter until the pandemic hit. Thankfully, our rural location allowed us to escape the city's restrictions and enjoy the outdoors. We reinvented playtime, creating new games and exploring every nook and cranny of our property.

Even during those times of despair, we made many cherished memories that carried us through the darkest of days. I have a vivid memory of a delightful evening when we gathered to play hide and seek on our family's old farmland. The property had an aging barn, which was used for storage. During this particular game, AJ decided to use this spot for hiding. He was particularly proud of his exceptional talent for hiding. He was bursting with excitement, having discovered the ultimate hiding spot that no one could uncover. To maintain the secrecy of his special spot, he insisted that everyone leave the barn before he emerged.

Another cherished memory takes me back to a stormy day when a fierce weather event had toppled some trees in our parents' yard. On a subsequent hide and seek session, AJ and I partnered up against Tim, Gavin, and Keegan. Among the fallen debris, two cypress trees stood in close proximity to each other. One remained upright while the other lay on the ground. I chose to venture into the hollow of the standing tree while AJ skillfully hid himself in the fallen one.

As the others tirelessly searched for us, we whispered quietly to each other, reveling in the thrill of our covert communication. Finally, when everyone accepted defeat, AJ and I emerged victorious. We couldn't contain our pride, knowing that we had discovered exceptional hiding spots.

Amidst these warm memories, the isolation took a toll on AJ's mental health. COVID had shut down schools, plunging us into a world of remote learning. While Tim and I continued working, my parents ensured the boys woke up, ate breakfast, and tackled their online studies.

During that period, AJ was primarily engaged in his individual online assignments. One day, he found himself in a Zoom session with his classmates. I happened to be around when his teacher posed a question, “Do you guys miss your teachers yet?”

Despite his love for socializing, AJ couldn't resist a cheeky response. He blurted out, "Nope, not at all!"

We knew better, of course. AJ thrived on being the class clown, the entertainer who craved recess and the company of his friends. The isolation, I believe, affected him more deeply than the others.

Despite having some awareness of the problems, I had no idea how deeply rooted they were. My sons were always energetic and joyful, a lively bunch. Our family appeared flawless, with memories of baseball games, hide-and-seek, and board games representing their childhood. Within our cozy home, life was magical. I have countless memories of those blissful days. Today, when I look back, they seem like a hazy dream in the sharp light of nightmarish reality. However, I will continue exploring the depths of those cherished recollections in honor of my beloved son.

CHAPTER TWO
The Light of AJ's Spirit

The absence of a loved one leaves a void, an ache that feels impossible to bear. Sometimes, this emptiness is so suffocating it threatens to drown you. After losing AJ, I also found myself succumbing to this darkness; however, the light of his spirit rescued me. I learned to navigate his absence by piecing together the fragments of his spirit. My mind has transformed into a scrapbook of his life, each page holding a memory of AJ, a reflection of his life. But my collection extends beyond the confines of my mind. I gather his essence from every soul he touched, every life he brightened, and find solace in their combined glow.

Luckily for me, AJ left a mark on everyone he met, so I have many stories to collect! Everyone describes him as a ray of sunshine. He was always ready for a good time and a laugh, but it wasn't just fun and games; he genuinely cared about making others feel good. The most remarkable thing everyone remembers about AJ is his smile. His ear-to-ear grin was warm and inviting, and if you weren't smiling back, he didn't hesitate to tell a quick joke or a funny story to lighten the mood. He wanted everyone to be as happy as he was.

Even at ten, AJ was different. Most kids his age were wrapped up in themselves, but not him. As I look back, I often find myself thinking how he was wise beyond his years. One day, while cleaning his room, I stumbled upon something he wrote that I'd never seen before a paragraph titled "What does it mean to be awesome?"

In his own words, AJ wrote: "The way I see it, awesome means to be smart, fun, playful, and just being yourself. You could also be kind and respectful to other people, be a good role model for others, be nice, be accepting, and just support other people when they are sad. Another way to be awesome is helping your community by doing things such as picking up trash and lots of other things."

He concluded with a powerful statement: "Don't let people change you." This simple sentence, coming from a ten-year-old, displayed a level of wisdom and understanding that many adults never grasp.

Throughout his life, his actions were a reflection of those profound words. He was a team player, always cheering his friends on and making sure everyone felt included. At school, he wouldn't just sit and learn. He'd help pick up after class, hold doors open, or stay late to clean with the teacher. On the bus, he always greeted the drivers with a good morning and wished them a good evening on his way home. They always greeted him with smiles, and everyone wanted to sit with him. He just had that way about him. His love wasn't just restricted to people. His friend's mom recalls a sleepover where AJ, noticing their cats, created a bed for one of them inside their tent. It was an example of his loving and protective nature that extended not just to people but to animals and everything around him.

AJ was a charmer, and all his teachers had stories. One remembers him as a sweet, energetic first-grader who loved sharing his knowledge (and making her laugh!) between dirt bike rides and hallway greetings. Another called him "sunshine" because he brightened her day with his genuine interest and willingness to chat.

"Whenever AJ was in my presence," she said, "he went out of his way to find me and speak to me. It was a privilege to have him as a student. He was a gift that kept on giving."

Beyond his smile, he had a unique sense of style, too. He rocked a good mohawk like no other, especially in kindergarten when his stood taller than anyone's ever seen in that school. He was always a conversation starter, turning heads wherever he went.

Then, in fourth grade, he was chosen as a graduation marshal for the fifth-grade ceremony, but his teacher warned him it was a serious event and he needed to act the part. I remember him practicing a few nights before. He put on his dress clothes – shirt and tie over pajamas – topped with bright yellow sunglasses. He struck a pose and demanded, "How's my outfit? Does this look appropriate for the day?" in his best Men in Black impression. He sent the picture to his teacher, and she couldn’t contain her laughter. Despite the silliness, it proved he could put away his smile when needed.

Even before kindergarten, in a program called "Britches and Braids," his librarian remembers him vividly. She recalls the teacher going around the room, asking each child to introduce themselves. And then, there it was, his sweet little voice ringing out, "My name's Meatball!"

Honestly, we still don't know how the nickname originated. Dad called him "Meatball" once, and somehow, it just stuck. From around four years old, he was Mighty Meatball. Even on his football support t-shirts, we had "Mighty Meat" proudly printed along with his number. His best friend, now 16, even got a tattoo – a smiling "Meatball" wearing sunglasses.

Another one of AJ's friends, Makynley, shared a memory with me that illustrates his kindness and ability to make people smile. In fifth grade, she was incredibly nervous about doing the morning announcements. She remembers barely being able to speak at first, so nervous she could barely talk.

When her mom picked her up that day, expecting a report on how it went, Makynley instead burst into laughter, tears welling up in her eyes. Her mom was understandably confused and asked, "What in the world is wrong with you?"

Makynley, still giggling, explained that right after starting the announcement, the principal told her to move closer to the microphone because she was too far away. But it wasn't that part that made her laugh.

Afterward, she saw AJ, and he, with his signature big smile, said, "You did really good! All I heard was, 'Good morning, this is Makynley,' and then you just went, pshhhshsshshs, like muffled sounds into the microphone."

Makynley remembers his humor instantly lifting her spirits, completely erasing her fear. It's a memory she cherishes and tells often, highlighting how AJ's smile could brighten anyone's day, even when they were feeling down. She also remembers his kindness, infectious laughter, and beautiful big blue eyes.

"I would give anything to hear him laugh just one more time," she said, her voice filled with warmth and longing.

Makynley also remembers asking AJ to play volleyball during recess. He usually preferred football, but nine times out of ten, he would eventually join her. Now, in a different school, she plays volleyball and wears a red jersey, AJ's favorite color.

He taught her the "floss" dance move, and she remembers how they would crack up together as he taught her. When she complained about being cold outside, he'd tell her, "Just run around; it'll warm you up!"

Another cherished memory was their fourth-grade field trip to the Wright Brothers museum. They ran around the whole time, pretending to be airplanes, their laughter echoing through the exhibits.

Makynley considers AJ her best friend, someone who will always hold a special place in her heart. "I miss him so much and can't wait to see him again," she said, her voice filled with emotion. Her mother even confided in me that she still talks to AJ regularly and tells her friends about him. She said he'll remain a part of her life forever. It is precious how much he meant to her in such a short time.

AJ wouldn't leave a single soul a stranger. No matter who you were, he'd strike up a conversation, bombarding you with questions about your life simply because he wanted to know you. Everyone he met became a friend.

There was my coworker's daughter, Reagan. When she started riding the bus to school, she spent some time at my mom's house, where mom helped with the school runs. Reagan wouldn't stop talking about AJ, so much so that her dad had to give her "the talk" about boys. But her mom knew AJ was always looking out for her. Reagan remembers him sitting with her, making sure she felt safe and knew where to go.

I have another story reflecting AJ's exceptional social skills. One day, my mom took the kids to a bounce house while they were out of school. My coworker, who happened to be there with her grandchildren, recognized them from Facebook pictures. She introduced herself to my mom, mentioning she worked with me and recognized the kids.

"Before I knew it," my coworker said with a laugh, "here come my grandson and AJ running around the corner, playing like they'd been best friends for years!" And there was AJ, with his signature smile and that sweet, polite personality.

While AJ loved spending time with his friends and having fun, he never forgot about his family. Even though boys can sometimes get totally wrapped up in their own adventures, AJ always made time for me as well. He loved our "mommy-son dates." He'd constantly ask, "When are we going to have a mommy-son date?" He loved me, and I loved him. AJ, like me, shared a deep connection with the ocean. He loved swimming, bodyboarding, and just being outdoors, embracing the fresh air and sunshine. The beach was definitely our happy place together.

Our family was big, playful, and competitive. We loved games and races, always pushing each other to be our best. One time, AJ's grandmother (Nene) was visiting. Out of nowhere, AJ got an idea in his head; he wanted to race her to my mom's house. Nene hesitated, obviously, saying she hadn't run in a while and wasn't sure how fast she'd be. AJ, with his sweet smile, encouraged her, "All you have to do, Nene, is believe in yourself, and you can do it!"

He proceeded to win the race, of course, but then followed it up with big hugs and laughter. He was fiercely competitive yet always caring and nurturing.

That playful spirit was evident in everything AJ did. Weekends at our family grounds were filled with the rambunctious energy of AJ, his cousin Brooke, and his brother Gavin. They spent countless weekends at our family grounds, exploring and getting into harmless mischief. Their adventures often involved four-wheelers and go-carts, especially after a rainy day that transformed the ground into a mud paradise. Mud pies, mud fights, and mud-slinging with the four-wheelers were their favorite messy activities. Some days, they were so caked in mud they needed to hose down before even considering stepping inside! At times, their harmless fun went a little too far. They'd catch frogs and toads, put them in a large pot, and dare each other to kiss them or poke them with sticks. With adult supervision, of course, they'd occasionally "liven things up" by throwing a firecracker in the pot. Tadpoles caught in the ditch met a similar fate. Once, they froze them, then dared each other to eat them. There was truly never a dull moment when these kids were playing outside.

Sometimes, his sense of humor left me concerned and amused in equal measure. One cookout, we had the grill fired up on the front porch, burgers sizzling, and hot dogs waiting their turn. My husband tossed the frozen hot dogs on the grill, and somehow, a grease fire erupted. He instinctively grabbed the water hose, unaware that it would only worsen things. Together with a friend, they heroically carried the flaming grill away from the porch, preventing disaster.

The hot dogs, needless to say, were burnt to a crisp. But AJ, ever the daredevil, blurted out, "Who dares me to eat one?" My husband, in a moment of amusement, offered him five dollars if he could stomach it.

So there he was the crazy little kid, holding a charred, charcoal-coated hot dog on a bun with ketchup and mustard. The look on his face as he tried to take a bite was priceless. He quickly realized it was a terrible decision, the crunch of the outside contrasting with the frozen center.

"It's so crispy on the outside, but it's still frozen in the middle!" he laughed, choking down a few bites before giving up, spitting it out, and begging for a drink.

"Only you," I said, shaking my head, amused. That was just AJ - always up for a laugh, even if it meant doing something ridiculous or eating something inedible. He found humor in the most unexpected places – sometimes, even in serious situations.

For instance, even during the pastor's serious sermon at church, AJ couldn't resist a joke. After a heavy message, the pastor asked for questions or comments. AJ raised his hand and chimed in, "Okay, when do we get the candy?"

His pastor called him a "sharp, perspective kid." There's another memory from church when an adult was teasing some of the kids. AJ looked right at him and said with a straight face, "I'm keeping my eye on you, sir!"

There was never a dull moment with AJ around. I remember one Christmas Eve, at my husband's family gathering, we were all gathered around, enjoying the holiday spirit. Dinner was finished, presents unwrapped, and the music started playing. With bellies full, everyone was too exhausted to hit the dance floor. That's when AJ found his groove. He took center stage on the dance floor, moving and shaking with an infectious energy that drew everyone in. I remember him and his grandpa having a little dance-off. I still have a video recording of that precious moment, and it still warms my heart.

Despite AJ's carefree attitude, he took things seriously when he needed to. His love for everything around him was matched only by his thirst for knowledge. From a young age, he was a bright kid. He consistently excelled in school, rarely receiving anything lower than a B. His intelligence was recognized in fifth grade when he was inducted into the Junior Beta Club, even becoming the vice president, thanks to his impressive second-highest average in the entire grade level. He was even part of the fifth-grade AIG (Academically and intellectually Gifted) program, something he truly enjoyed. I honestly never knew about his involvement in creating and coding a Sphero robot at school. He was even chosen to write about it for the Buckland Gates on the Go AIG website. After AJ passed away, his teacher shared his favorite part about being in the program: practicing flying hoops and landing the Sphero through them, all without turning it off. He learned how to change the battery, operate the drone better, and navigate it, even coaching others on how to fly. "My favorite part," AJ wrote, "is being able to help the person flying the drone land and go through the hoops."

Despite his achievements, AJ never boasted. He was known for his modesty. This applied to athletics, too. He started playing football in third grade, transforming into a different force on the field, as his coach playfully remarked. Though AJ brushed off the compliments, he did lead with a calm demeanor that switched to fierce determination under his helmet. His coach said that AJ transformed into a beast on the field.

One defining moment was the championship game. The team was struggling, and everyone was asking, "Where's AJ? We need him!" When he finally entered the field, he rallied his teammates, and they ended up winning by a landslide. His coach called him "one heck of a baller," but AJ saw himself as a leader, both on and off the field.

Baseball was no different. Initially, he could only manage weak grounders, but then something clicked, and he started hitting booming shots to the outfield. Being a lefty, he surprised everyone with his powerful hits. Reaching base, a wide grin would spread across his face, sometimes even surprised at his own accomplishment. He was simply proud of himself.

AJ had an incredible zest for life. He was an infectious burst of sunshine who brightened every room he entered - always curious, always smiling. For someone who embraced life so whole-heartedly, it’s a tragedy that he's not around anymore. He saw beauty in every detail, from finding bugs to play with and calling them his friends to his mischievous pranks that never failed to bring laughter. So, whenever grief washes over me, I find solace flipping through the scrapbook of AJ's stories, a collection woven with love from all who knew him.

CHAPTER THREE
The Day Everything Changed

Have you ever encountered a moment that cleaved your life in two, carving a chasm between the before and the after? For some, such a moment might be a triumph, a glorious union like the forging of a lifelong bond. But for me, the seismic shift that irrevocably altered the essence of my existence arrived on the day my son took his own life. It was as if the very fabric of reality tore asunder, leaving behind a world forever changed, its colors dulled, and its melody forever muted.

It started off as just another Monday, the kind that starts with the jarring beep of the alarm at 4:15 am. I dragged myself out of bed, already feeling the weight of the upcoming week settling in my bones. The house was quiet; everyone was still nestled in their own dreams. I tiptoed past Gavin and Keegan's rooms, planting a kiss on their foreheads as I did every morning. AJ was on the couch, a familiar sight since he often spent the night there.

At work, the day unfolded in a predictable rhythm. I sent my usual 6:30 am text to my husband, wishing him a good day. Around 9:00 am, I reached out to Gavin as he was the eldest. "Good morning, sunshine! Just checking in, love you and have a great day!" I hit send and returned to the tasks of the day.

To my relief, work ended a bit early. I stopped by the store, grabbing snacks and lunches for the kids. Pulling into the driveway, a sense of relief washed over me. I reached for my phone, checking a voicemail while grabbing my lunchbox from the passenger seat. As I popped open the back door, a commotion from the front of the house sent a jolt of fear through me.

My heart hammering against my ribs, I raced around the house. There, I caught sight of Gavin, but he was a blur of motion sprinting toward my parents' house next door. He was yelling, but his words were lost in the wind. Panic clawed at my throat. "Gavin!" I screamed. But he was gone, disappearing behind the open door of my parents' house.

I followed him as fast as my feet could carry me. Reaching the doorway, I found my parents with Gavin, his face streaked with tears. "What's wrong?" I gasped.

The panic in Gavin's voice echoed through my ears as he repeated, "He's in your room, he's in your room."

I didn't understand. Confusion battled against a rising tide of fear. Who? What? But the raw terror in his eyes hinted at something I couldn't begin to imagine.

My groceries clattered to the ground, forgotten. I sprinted toward the front door, my vision blurring at the edges. Reaching the living room, I saw the office door ajar, revealing a horrifying scene. My breath caught in my throat. AJ. He was sprawled on the floor at the foot of my bed, his body unnaturally still.

A primal scream ripped from my throat. "AJ!" I roared. My legs propelled me forward. Upon reaching the bedroom door, I saw him clearly; he was bathed in an unsettling pool of red. At first, I thought that maybe he had fallen and hit his head on the baseboard because he was lying right up against it. He was still breathing. I checked for a pulse, and he still had one.

"AJ!" I called out to him.

The world dissolved into chaos. All I remember is collapsing beside him, screaming his name, pleading with him to respond. My own voice sounded foreign. My mind refused to process the sight before me.

Through the haze of terror, I remember my mother and son rushing in. My mother's scream pierced the air, a sound that mirrored the agony twisting in my gut. We called 911. Thankfully, amidst the pandemonium, Keegan remained oblivious, napping peacefully on the other side of the house. My stepfather mercifully took him away, sparing him from witnessing the nightmare unfolding before me.

The world dissolved into a chaotic blur. Sirens wailed in the distance, growing closer with each passing moment. Faces swam in and out of focus, their voices merely a muffled hum against the pounding in my ears. My body moved mechanically; I was numb and disconnected from the unfolding scene. Paramedics swarmed the room and whisked AJ away. I barely registered the gun lying near him, the shock still holding me captive in a state of horrified disbelief. My mind was a storm of unanswered questions. How? How could this be? How could this have happened? Why on earth did he have a gun? We have always emphasized gun safety and the dangers of playing with firearms. Just a week or so before, my husband had taken the gun out and shown it to them. We discussed the current uncertain times, and they all knew where the gun was kept. They had received training in target shooting gun safety and practiced handling it. They understood that it was for protection if someone were to enter the house. So, I couldn't, for the life of me, understand why he would have gotten it. It had been just another ordinary Monday, a routine day like any other. Yet, here I was, the weight of the world pressing down on my chest.

The initial plan for a specialized transport team fell through. I remember the Nightingale was supposed to come but then they didn’t. As they loaded him into the ambulance without me, I felt a growing sense of panic. I begged one of the sheriff's deputies at that time to let me ride with AJ, but they wouldn't let me. I didn’t want my baby boy out of my sight. My cousin took charge and drove me and Tim to the CHKD where they'd told us AJ was headed.

However, fate had a different path in store. The jarring ring of the phone sliced through the tense silence in the car. It was the hospital; they were having trouble with AJ, and they had to take him to Obici to stabilize him.

We executed a frantic U-turn. Every passing second felt like an eternity; as we pulled into the familiar parking lot of Obici, a sickening sense of foreboding washed over me. This wasn't supposed to happen. This was the place where I cared for others, not the place where I feared for my own child.

Bursting through ER frantically, I felt a primal urge to reach AJ, to hold him close and chase away whatever demons he was battling. Tears welled up in my eyes, blurring the world around me.

My voice cracked as I explained the situation, desperation lacing each word. Then, a familiar face appeared, her eyes meeting mine. It was Kellin, the hospital chaplain. Since we worked together, she knew me and as she realized it was my son struggling to survive, she enveloped me in a tight hug. The warmth of her embrace offered a momentary respite from the icy grip of fear. She ushered us into a quiet room, away from the controlled chaos of the emergency room. My husband and I clung to each other, seeking strength in the shared silence.

Finally, a doctor appeared, his words carrying the weight of both relief and the unknown. They had stabilized AJ, he informed us, and he was being transferred to CHKD, a children's hospital better equipped to handle his case.

The wait for the ambulance felt like an eternity. Finally, it arrived and as we stepped inside, the sterile white walls did little to dispel the suffocating fear. My gaze fell upon AJ, his small form dwarfed by the gurney. The sight of him, my sweet boy, vulnerable with a breathing tube coming out of his mouth and his head swathed in gauze, ripped a fresh wave of agony through me.

I grasped his tiny hand, its coolness sending shivers down my spine. "Stay with me, baby," I pleaded. "Don't leave me."

Despite being allowed to ride with AJ, regulations placed me in the front, separated from him by a thin partition and the relentless hum of the engine. My cousin followed behind with my husband.

Reaching AJ's side, I leaned down, brushing my lips against his forehead. "It's okay, baby," I whispered, my voice trembling. "Mama's here." His alarmingly high heart rate had dipped to a concerningly low level. The clinical part of me, the nurse trained to remain calm under pressure, recognized the ominous sign.

I barely remember the ride to the hospital. I recall one of my best friend's moms, who happens to be a member of EMS in Gates County, where we live, called me because she had missed several calls from me. I was trying to reach her on the way to the hospital for any updates on AJ's condition. She called me back while we were en route to the children's hospital and expressed her apologies for missing my calls. We discussed the situation, and she shared some of the details they had observed at the scene. She advised me to prepare myself to make some difficult decisions. I expressed my uncertainty, but we were arriving at the hospital, so I had to cut the conversation short.

After parking, I was allowed to see him briefly, just for a moment, through a small window. I told him that it was going to be okay.

Following him into the ER, I was stopped abruptly in the hallway as they rushed him behind a curtain. I was left alone. Muffled shouts and the frantic beeping of machines filtered through the thin curtain.

Then, the dreaded words echoed from behind the barrier. "Code Blue!" My breath hitched in my throat, the world tilting on its axis. Every fiber of my being screamed in denial as I sank to my knees, a guttural cry escaping my lips.

Just then, Tim burst through the doors, his face etched with worry. The doctor emerged from behind the curtain. His somber expression was enough to confirm my worst fears. "He's gone," he said gently. The world dissolved into a blur of grief; my sweet AJ was gone.

At that point, I felt as though my heart was ripped from my chest.

The news hit me like a physical blow. The air seemed to leave the room, and I struggled to breathe. They finally allowed Tim and me to see him. My beautiful boy, usually so full of life, lay there pale and unmoving. It felt like a scene from a bad dream, a cruel twist of reality.

Ignoring the sterile smell of the hospital room, I crawled onto the stretcher beside him. Tears streamed down my face as I wrapped my arms around his small, fragile body. Everything else faded away – the hushed voices, the beeping machines, the concerned faces of the doctors - all I felt was the overwhelming weight of grief.

Minutes bled into an eternity as I clung to him, whispering choked goodbyes and promises I couldn't keep. The time came when they gently but firmly asked me to let go. It was the hardest thing I'd ever done.

Numb and speechless, Tim and I sat together, the shared pain hanging heavy in the air. We called for a ride, but the familiar comfort of my brother-in-law's presence did nothing to penetrate the fog of grief. On the car ride home, I stared out the window, the world blurring past my tear-filled eyes.

Stepping back into the house, I was met with a wave of well-meaning faces. Family and friends offered their condolences. Over the next few days, the house remained a constant thrum of activity. A constant stream of visitors filled the house, food piled up on the counters, untouched. All I craved was silence, a moment to breathe and process the unimaginable pain.

Friday arrived as a cruel reminder of what should have been. It was supposed to be AJ's 11th birthday, a day filled with laughter, cake, and the joyful chaos of a child's celebration. Instead, we were finalizing funeral arrangements.

Later that afternoon, we were ushered outside. As we reached the end of the driveway, a sight unfolded that brought tears to my eyes. A yellow school bus stood proudly at the head of a line of cars, the flashing lights of the sheriff's vehicle leading the way. Our community, in a beautiful display of compassion, had organized a surprise parade in AJ's honor. Bus drivers, teachers, and friends lined the street, holding balloons, flowers, and handmade posters. Each held a message of love and support, reflecting the impact AJ had on their lives. At that moment, the suffocating weight of grief lifted slightly. The outpouring of love from our community was a reminder that we weren't alone. My family was blown away by the display of love and support.

Due to the pandemic, we couldn't have a traditional service, so we decided to hold a celebration of life at home. Since we weren't a religious family, finding an officiant was a challenge. My mom suggested her pastor, but I just didn't resonate with that idea. I wanted it to be someone who personally knew my son. Then, a deputy named Pastor Jordan, who had been with us throughout that difficult week, offered to officiate, and his genuine support sealed the deal.

When Saturday came, it felt like a day I had barely agreed to. Getting ready felt like going through the motions; the full weight of the situation hadn't sunk in yet. Thankfully, our friends and family took charge of the logistics for the day. I honestly couldn't have done it without their help.

Our home, usually filled with laughter and the sound of AJ's playful spirit, became a space of shared grief. Hundreds of people gathered. The room was filled with flowers and trees meant for our memorial garden, bringing color and life to the somber atmosphere. A friend's music played softly as Pastor Jordan delivered a heartfelt tribute to AJ. Others shared their favorite memories, painting a vivid picture of his bright spirit. Finally, we all wrote messages on balloons, each carrying a piece of our love, and released them into the sky. It was a beautiful tribute, a bittersweet farewell to my precious son.

Sunday brought a fresh wave of emotions. It was Mother's Day, and it was now tainted by this unimaginable loss. This week had been a relentless assault on my soul – AJ's passing, his birthday overshadowed by grief, and now this, as family members said their goodbyes and departed, a different kind of emptiness settled in. The constant activity and well-meaning voices had acted as a shield - a buffer against the raw grief. Now, left alone with the deafening silence, I wasn't sure which was worse – the overwhelming stimulation or the crushing loneliness that threatened to consume me.

After everyone left, my husband stayed home with me for another week or so. However, he doesn't handle idleness well, so he went back to work to keep his mind occupied. I, on the other hand, remained at home for a much longer period.

Once my mother-in-law left to return to Ohio, the silence and emptiness of the house became overwhelming. We were there for each other, but grief left us speechless and confused. Even today, my heart and mind battle constantly.

My heart remembers AJ's happiness and outgoing personality. He never showed any signs of sadness or suicidal intent. But my logical side, my brain, can't reconcile that with the reality of what happened. Why else would he have had a gun?

Looking back, my husband and I discussed subtle changes we noticed in AJ. He had been quieter on some days, less talkative. We tried to talk to him, but he always insisted everything was alright. Then, he'd go back to his usual playful self and crack a joke. We didn't think much of it at the time.

I keep asking myself: "What did I miss? How did this happen? What could I have done differently?" My friend, whose son was AJ's best friend, shared my confusion. She assured me I hadn't missed anything and that she doesn't believe it was intentional. If I had missed the signs, she argued, then all of us had. We understand what happened, but to this day, our hearts still struggle to accept it.

CHAPTER FOUR
Navigating Grief and Loss

The absence of your loved ones cuts so deep it carves a raw wound in the depths of your soul. Its relentless presence seeps through every fiber of being, refusing to be ignored. Even when one attempts to numb the ache, it lingers, impossible to escape. After losing my precious son, grief has become a pervasive companion, forever occupying the space that my AJ once filled. People often speak of the tragedy, acknowledging the profound loss I have endured. But it is coming to terms with this devastating absence that inflicts its own unique trauma. It is a painful journey that I had not anticipated, one that I could never have prepared for. It is a journey that began the moment I laid eyes upon my son's lifeless body, and it persists to this very day.

Bearing the weight of this unfathomable loss, the initial shock began to recede, replaced by a suffocating sense of quiet despair. In the aftermath, an air of solemnity settled upon our household. The funeral service had concluded, and as the majority of mourners departed, only a small group of cousins remained. In an attempt to lift our spirits, some of our cousins proposed a game of kickball in the front yard. My husband agreed, suggesting that a breath of fresh air might be exactly what we need. Outside, in the expanse of our front yard, we found ourselves surrounded by the beauty of nature. Birds of various species fluttered about, and their melodies mingled with the heavy silence that hung in the air. Despite the overwhelming sorrow, we felt a sense of calm.

Suddenly, a small bird caught our attention - a vibrant blue parakeet perched on a nearby tree. Curiosity compelled us to approach cautiously, as if afraid the bird might vanish into thin air. To our amazement, it allowed my husband to draw near, extending his hand to cradle the delicate creature. In that tender moment, I felt something profound I couldn't quite understand.

I noticed that the parakeet bore a band - a sign that it belonged to someone. So, I turned to social media to seek answers, posting a query about a lost bird. The responses poured in, each one carrying a glimmer of hope. I learned something new: parakeets are considered as messengers from heaven.

A friend of mine was a veterinary technician who examined the bird and confirmed its gender. It was a male - a little boy! That newfound knowledge seemed to deepen the significance. It was as if our son, in some ethereal form, had chosen this avian guise to communicate with us - to assure us that he was safe and at peace. Through tear-filled eyes, we marveled at this extraordinary occurrence.

Yet, as the weeks crawled by, the initial spark of hope began to dwindle. The overwhelming reality of our loss settled in with renewed intensity. Before I knew it, two whole months had bled by since the world had tilted on its axis. It was just me and my two boys at home. Tim had returned to work, leaving me to navigate the profound emptiness that permeated our once-vibrant household. My mother-in-law stayed with us briefly, but eventually, she had to return to her own life and responsibilities.

The room where we had found AJ lifeless became a constant reminder of our loss. Every time I stepped foot into that bedroom, all I could see was his lifeless form, and the overwhelming feeling of helplessness washed over me. As both a mother and a nurse, not being able to save the life that mattered most to me was a deep wound that seemed impossible to heal.

Sleeping in our bedroom became unbearable. The memory of that tragic day was etched into every corner of the room. We couldn't bear to be surrounded by those haunting images. Generous friends bought us an air mattress, and we found solace in sleeping in the living room instead. It took months, perhaps even longer, before we mustered the courage to reclaim our bedroom and restore some semblance of normalcy.

The sight of the carpet, stained with blood from AJ's final moments, was a painful reminder of our loss. Despite the efforts of our family members to clean it, the stains remained. In the end, they had no choice but to cut out a large square of carpet, leaving a bare patch that extended from our bedroom into the adjacent sitting room. It was a visual representation of the void left in our lives. There were times when I couldn't resist the urge to lay on that very spot where AJ had taken his last breath. It was as if being close to that space would somehow bring me closer to him. Sometimes, I found myself there without even consciously deciding to do so. Grief has a way of guiding our actions, even when our minds are lost in a haze of sorrow.

Every morning felt like a daunting roller coaster ride as I struggled to find the strength to get out of bed and face the day alongside my two boys and Tim. It was a constant battle, and there were times when all I wanted was to stay cocooned in the comfort of my sheets, to simply not wake up. But deep down, I knew that wasn't an option. I had a responsibility to my children, who needed me now more than ever, and a family that relied on me to keep things together.

In those early days, two of my friends became my pillars of support. They went above and beyond, stepping into the role of family by making regular visits to my home. At first, it was once a week, but as time went on, they came every couple of weeks. Their presence brought a sense of solace to my shattered world. They would arrive with homemade dinners, and we would gather together on Friday evenings, allowing me the space to talk or simply forget about my troubles, even if only for a little while. Those moments were a lifeline. Those two friends, who had become like family, kept me going. Their support, alongside the love of my boys and husband, gave me the strength to carry on. In a busy world where friendships often take a back seat, these two individuals consistently proved their commitment to me. They were there for me every step of the way, providing whatever I needed, and for that, I will forever be grateful.

Occasionally, I would find myself caught up in their company, distracted from the weight of my grief. In those fleeting moments, a smile would grace my face, or even a laugh would escape my lips. However, these seemingly trivial occurrences sent a jolt of guilt coursing through me. How could I allow myself these glimpses of joy when AJ was gone? But deep down, I knew that AJ, my loved one, would never want me to be consumed by sorrow and tears. So, I tried my best to stay present in those moments, cherishing the respite they provided.

Despite the support I was receiving, I found it incredibly challenging to get back on my feet. During those few months, I could only find comfort within the confines of my home, away from the demands of work. Throughout this period, my boss proved to be incredible! She reached out to me frequently, not to pressure me into returning to work, but simply to check in and see how I was coping. She genuinely cared for my well-being and offered her assistance in any way she could. Deep down, I knew that I wasn't mentally prepared to resume my responsibilities in patient care. The mere thought of shouldering that level of responsibility again weighed heavily on my mind. How could I nurse someone else when I couldn't save my son? This question haunted me.

Understanding my predicament, my boss presented me with an alternative. She told me that whenever I felt ready, I could return to the hospital, even if it was just to escape the confines of my house for a little while. She mentioned the pass office, where they handled charts for upcoming surgeries. The staff there would call patients, review their medical history and medications, and provide them with their arrival times. It seemed like a gentle way for me to ease back into the workforce. I agreed to start with just two days a week. I hoped that it would help me regain a sense of regularity and human interaction.

In the beginning, my tasks were simple, mostly involving organizing and assembling charts. I took small steps, gradually immersing myself in patient phone calls and other related responsibilities. It took about another month or two before I returned to my actual department in outpatient surgery. Stepping back into that environment was a roller coaster of emotions. I was greeted by coworkers I hadn't seen in months, all of them eager to embrace me, talk to me, and ensure that I was doing okay.

Before I officially returned, my boss had asked me how I wanted to handle my comeback. She shared an example of a doctor whose wife had passed away and how he preferred not to discuss it. She gave me the option to keep things strictly professional, with no questions asked, or to allow people to approach me and inquire about my experience. I didn't know exactly how to answer that question. Each day was different for me, and my emotions fluctuated. There were times when I yearned to talk about my loss, while other times, I just wanted everyone to leave me be.

On my first day back, a few coworkers approached me and enveloped me in warm hugs. In those moments, I couldn't help but feel overwhelmed, and tears streamed down my face once again. It was a struggle to move forward with my own life while recognizing that the life of someone I love more than life itself had come to an end. However, throughout this emotional turmoil, my colleagues surrounded me with love and support.

They could sense when I needed a moment to myself. If they saw that look on my face, they kindly allowed me to retreat to the break room to collect myself or shed a few tears. Sometimes, they would join me and initiate conversation if I felt up to it. Other times, they would silently sit beside me, offering their quiet presence as a source of comfort. They were exceptional in their efforts to ease me back into the rhythm of work each day. I suppose, due to my state of mind, they had to walk on eggshells around me. They delicately navigated around me, aware of the unpredictability of my emotions. Yet, they handled it all with grace.

Every day, as I walked into the hospital, I felt a piercing vulnerability deep within. But I remained determined to push through, to put on a brave face, and to carry on with my work. Eventually, I discovered the art of concealing my emotions, carefully guarding them behind a mask of strength. It was a skill that I learned over time, but it was never an easy task. Even to this day, there are moments that weigh heavier on my heart than others. The most challenging aspect of being back at work and caring for patients lies in making small talk and building connections. It's those innocent questions like "How many children do you have?" that send me into a whirlwind of conflicting emotions. How do I answer that? Do I reveal the truth that I had three boys but tragically lost one? Or do I brush it off with a simple response, saying I have two boys at home? It's a difficult topic for me to broach with strangers, and I find myself grappling with the answer no matter how many times I've been asked this simple question. I didn't necessarily want to divulge the heart-wrenching details of what had transpired. I wasn't ready to immerse myself in an emotional battle zone where I'd have to recount the painful events. Therefore, navigating the path back to a regular, everyday routine proved to be an arduous task.

For me, time itself had become a confounding entity. Every waking moment felt surreal – like a dream or a nightmare. There were moments that felt as if everything had happened just yesterday, while others felt like distant memories rushing by in a blur. It was as if several months of 2020 had vanished into thin air. I found myself constantly relying on calendars to even determine what day or month it was. The struggle was real.

As a nurse, part of my responsibility was to ask patients their orientation questions: who they were, where they were, and what day it was. But how could I pose those inquiries when I couldn't answer them myself on certain days? Sometimes, there were also instances where doubt crept in. Although others were understanding of my circumstances, I couldn't go too easily on myself. Oftentimes, I questioned my own capabilities. Could I still be a nurse? How could I care for others when I let down one of the most important people in my life? The struggle was a constant companion, a weight upon my shoulders. As time progressed, I suppose it did become somewhat easier to push those haunting thoughts to the back of my mind and maintain composure at work.

During these times, I must acknowledge the succor I received from my unit coordinator during those months. She possessed a keen ability to recognize when I was having a particularly rough day. On lighter days, she would simply glance at me and ask, "Do you want to go home?" To which

I would nod, my eyes filled with gratitude. She understood and allowed me the time I needed to piece my life back together.

Looking back, I realized that the timing of my transfer to the outpatient surgery department in 2019 was nothing short of divine intervention. It was as if God knew that remaining in the intensive care unit would have been too much for me during that time of grief and loss. I doubt I would have mustered the strength to return to work. I even contemplated leaving the nursing profession altogether. The departmental change was a true blessing, aligning perfectly with the events that unfolded.

By the end of that challenging year, I found myself back to working full-time hours in my department. I was fortunate to have a boss who understood the gravity of my situation. I was back on my feet, but on days when the weight of my emotions became too much to bear, she granted me permission to go home early. Retreating to the comfort of my own space, I would allow the tears to flow freely. However, I made sure to shield my children from witnessing my struggles, as I wanted to be their pillar of strength during their own vulnerable moments.

In these dark times, we all tried to be there for each other. Fortunately, my husband and I experienced contrasting days where we encountered our individual moments of despair. It allowed us to support one another and care for our children while the other was struggling. Our household truly became a remarkable display of teamwork. Eventually, I reached a point where I embraced the idea of letting our children witness my tears. I understood that by demonstrating my vulnerability and openly discussing my emotions, they would be more inclined to express their own feelings and ease their burdens.

In my upbringing, discussions about our problems were nonexistent. I suppressed them until I could no longer bear the weight. I was determined not to pass on this unhealthy habit to my children. I knew

I had to set an example for them, guiding them toward healing by encouraging open dialogue and discouraging the practice of bottling up emotions. Keeping those inner struggles concealed only leads to emotional and mental deterioration. It was about a month into our journey when we finally sought counseling.

Initially, we relied on online sessions as it was the only option available to us at the time. Gradually, my sons and I transitioned to in-person counseling sessions, while my husband, due to his work schedule, continued with online sessions for a little while longer.

Around four to six months into the process, my eldest son, Gavin, approached me and expressed his desire to discontinue counseling. I assured him that if he genuinely felt he was okay, I respected his decision. However, I made him promise that if he ever felt the need to return, he would reach out, and we would support him. I emphasized the importance of finding someone trustworthy to confide in. I reminded him, "If things get difficult, talk to someone, whether it be a friend, a teacher, or a counselor!" Even jotting down his thoughts on a piece of paper, and if he wished, tearing it up and discarding it could provide a sense of release. He gave me his word, promising to honor our agreement. Following his counseling journey, Gavin did really well.

On the other hand, Keegan showed more challenges. Being five years old, he struggled to comprehend the situation. Falling asleep one day with two brothers and waking up with just one was a bewildering experience for him. Processing such a profound loss proved immensely difficult. Consequently, we encountered behavioral issues and a barrage of questions. Keegan's delicate nature necessitated that he continue counseling alongside me for a while longer. However, after several months, we began to witness signs of improvement. Gradually, we allowed him to gradually decrease his counseling sessions, guiding him back into the routine of school and everyday life.

The adjustment period was arduous. In the beginning, we grappled with the question of how much we should discuss the situation. Were we talking about it too much or not enough? It felt like navigating a tightrope, delicately balancing the emotions of each family member. Undoubtedly, it was an exceedingly challenging time.

Personally, I underwent the most extensive counseling, attending sessions for about a year. Every single day, without fail, I found myself grappling with a multitude of haunting questions. What if there was something I missed? Could I have done things differently? I couldn't help but wonder if I had hurried home sooner or if I had pried more into AJ's quiet moments, maybe, just maybe, he would have opened up to me.

Even after countless counseling sessions, I struggled to come to terms with my loss. I didn't know how to cope – how to process the turmoil within. Day after day, a singular thought predominated my mind – I want AJ back. What in the world I wouldn't give to hold him just once again, to talk to him again? Overcome by anguish, I took to journaling and wrote AJ a letter.

It began like, *"I remember in the beginning everything felt so surreal - like one day I was just going to wake up, and it would all turn out to be a terrible dream. Some days, I find myself looking for you, eagerly waiting for you to come walking through the door. But the horrible reality is that you're gone - not ever coming back.*

After some weeks had passed, you came to visit from the other side. One night, I had a dream where you walked through the front door, and I just stood there and looked at you in disbelief. You asked me, 'Why are you looking at me like that?' I just ran to you and wrapped my arms around you.

But as soon as I pulled you close, you vanished into thin air. I remember waking up crying.

Another night, I had a dream where you came into the house and said, "Hey, Mama." I hugged you tight, and you told me you were sorry you couldn't stay, but you wanted me to know you were ok. While those dreams felt like such a tease, I also felt like you were trying to let me know you were still here with me. They brought me the tiniest bit of peace, even if just for a moment.

Sometimes, while I'm alone in the house, I hear the occasional footsteps or feel a cool presence surrounding me. I know these are signs that you are here. Call me crazy, but I've wanted to talk to you so badly that I've met with several mediums. I've gotten involved in things I never believed in. It's funny; I always thought they were such a scam. But I desperately needed to hear from you, so I gave it a try. Several people had told me that psychics/mediums were the devil's work and that I should stay far away from them. However, I had to try.

Each of them has told me things that they had no means of knowing. Each visit with a medium has brought me a valuable message – something I desperately needed. I remember opening up to the last one I visited. I told her how I just needed a hug from you. Just then, my friend's dog burst into the room, jumped into my lap, and threw her paws over my shoulders. It felt as though the little dog was delivering your hug. I just hugged her back as tightly as I could while silent tears ran down my cheeks.

Some days, I just sit and talk to you as if you were right next to me. Although I know you can't answer me, I know for sure that you can hear me. I took comfort in this knowledge alone.

We are getting so close to yet another missed birthday. This year, you will be turning 15. I often wonder how you'd have liked to spend your birthday, how tall you would be, and how that sweet voice would sound like now. I have no doubt that you would be as big as me now, if not bigger. When I watch your brothers out here riding dirt bikes and playing airsoft matches, I often remark that you should be here, playing along. If you were, I know you'd be giving them hell.

I think one of the hardest parts of you not being here is that Keegan doesn't get to know you. You left us so early that he barely has any memories of you. That breaks my heart more than one could ever know. He doesn't get to know how truly awesome you were. He actually reminds me a lot of you. The two of you resemble each other in looks, and he has mastered some of your facial expressions. He often also tells jokes that remind me of something you would say.

Gavin thinks of you often, reminding me of fun memories that have somehow escaped my mind. I wonder if you two would still be as close as you were growing up. Losing you has made me feel like such a failure as a mother. I should have been there more for you. I should have been able to save you. Now, as I try to make great memories with your brothers, I wish that you were here to enjoy all the things life has yet to offer us."

As I penned down each word of this letter, it offered a form of release. Yet, I couldn't make peace with this dreadful nightmare. Every day, I clung to his memories like a lifeline, but they haunted me just the same. I remember how he used to repeatedly ask, "When are we going to have a mommy and AJ day?" The guilt weighs heavily on me now, knowing that I didn't prioritize that special time with him. Perhaps, in those moments, he would have found the courage to share his thoughts and his struggles. It's an agonizing thought, one that will forever haunt me, for I will never have the answers I so desperately seek.

Carrying this burden of remorse and unanswered questions has become a part of my daily existence. Even after nearly four years have passed, the weight of it all remains. I often contemplate whether finding the answers to my questions would truly make a difference. Would it bring AJ back? No, I know deep down that it wouldn't. The truth is, I may never find that peace, that closure, and I'm forced to come to terms with that.

Attending counseling sessions, my husband and I had countless conversations about the purpose behind our tragedy. Why did we go through something so gut-wrenching? There had to be a reason. We both sensed that there was something we were meant to do with this unimaginable loss. A calling that tugged at our hearts, urging us to transform our pain into something meaningful. A that time, we had no inkling of what that something could be.

CHAPTER FIVE

Honoring AJ's Legacy

The memories of a loved one lost are a bittersweet paradox. They hold the power to pierce the soul, leaving raw wounds that seem impossible to heal. Yet, these same memories can be a source of immense strength. Losing a child intensifies this paradox to an unimaginable degree. No parent should have to endure such a profound, soul-crushing grief.

After my son's passing, I found myself adrift in a sea of uncharted emotions. The pain was like an overwhelming wave, threatening to drown me. I grappled with feelings I never knew existed. But even in this storm of despair, a flicker of resilience ignited within me. It was a strength buried deep - a wellspring I never knew I possessed.

This newfound strength stemmed from the boundless love I held for my son. His memory became a guiding light in the suffocating darkness, leading me through the most harrowing nights and the most dreary days. To truly honor him, I realized I needed to find the courage to rebuild myself. It wasn't just for my own sake but for my other children who needed their mother. Each day, I took a small step forward to reclaim the shattered pieces of myself. I began to cherish the memories of my son, not as instruments of torture but as evidence of a love that transcended even loss. Slowly, the sharp edges of grief softened, replaced by a bittersweet comfort – a reminder of the joy he brought into my life.

For a while, I blindly searched for that sense of purpose. However, Tim and I felt a strong urge to take action after losing AJ, even before we figured out what that action should be. We just wanted to help others find a way out of this nightmare. We discussed creating a program, perhaps similar to a big brother/big sister one, but existing programs already served that purpose. Our goal was to prevent others from experiencing the same pain we did.

The outpouring of support from friends and family included a sizeable donation fund. We were incredibly grateful for their generosity. We covered AJ's funeral expenses and created a memorial garden in his honor. The remaining funds sparked a desire within us – a desire to make a positive impact using the resources entrusted to us.

Thus, a year after our loss, Tim and I decided to channel our grief into something positive by creating a scholarship in AJ's memory. The town's school board, recognizing our heartache, offered invaluable support in making this vision a reality. Their non-profit status allowed us to establish a dedicated fund at their bank, ensuring the scholarship's long-term sustainability.

Designing the scholarship criteria was a way for us to keep AJ's spirit alive. While academic achievement was important, it wasn't the sole factor. We envisioned the scholarship going to students who mirrored AJ's well-rounded personality. A high GPA was a plus, but an active role in the community and a strong moral compass were equally important. In our minds, the ideal recipient would be someone who excelled in academics, gave back to their surroundings, and demonstrated the same positive character traits that we cherished in our son.

In May 2021, the scholarship found its first perfect recipient – a Gates County senior who wasn't just a leader but also embodied the kindness, compassion, hard work, and determination that we remembered so vividly in AJ. Her application stood out from the rest; it was almost as if AJ himself had chosen her. She wasn't just focused on academic achievement but also on making a positive impact in her community, just like AJ had. This resonated deeply with us, and we knew we had found someone who truly embodied AJ's spirit.

Since then, the scholarship has continued to grow and flourish, just like the love we have for AJ. As of May 2024, we've awarded a total of $10,000 across five scholarships, impacting the lives of deserving students. We've also begun adding a few extras to the scholarship package, like tumblers with the slogan "Grin Like AJ" – a constant reminder of our son's infectious smile – and even some laptops to help recipients with their studies. These additional resources are our way of giving back even more and ensuring that the scholarship continues to make a meaningful difference in the lives of deserving students.

Witnessing the positive impact of the scholarship on these deserving students further solidified our commitment to mental health advocacy. This realization led to the creation of Shine Through, a nonprofit organization dedicated to empowering youth and fostering a brighter future in mental wellness. Shine Through is a beacon of hope that reminds us that even in life's darkest moments, we have the power to choose to shine.

At Shine Through, we believe that mental illness shouldn't be a shroud of silence and shame. Shine Through operates on a three-pronged approach: education, advocacy, and empowerment. We strive to educate communities about mental health, dismantling the stigma and fostering open conversations. Through advocacy efforts, we push for policies and resources that prioritize youth mental well-being. Finally, Shine Through actively funds programs that equip young people with the tools and resources they need to navigate challenges and build emotional resilience. By supporting these programs, we invest in a future where mental health is understood, respected, and nurtured.

We saw firsthand the devastating consequences of mental health struggles left unaddressed. Witnessing the silence and shame surrounding these issues solidified our belief that change was needed. After enduring a gut-wrenching tragedy, it is nearly impossible to think beyond your own losses. For me, there has been nothing more brutal than coming to terms with AJ's suicide. The idea that my innocent child could be lost to such darkness remained unfathomable to me for a long time. My heart still grapples with the truth, but logic has finally caught up. This experience has propelled me on a quest to understand mental health and suicide. It has become my mission to break down the stigma surrounding mental health issues. I devoured webinars and classes, learning the intricacies of the brain and its connection to mental well-being.

Driven by a desire to make a difference, I joined the American Foundation for Suicide Prevention (AFSP) and trained to become a presenter. But I craved a deeper impact. I enrolled in courses to become a mental health coach, aiming to help both adults and young people navigate their emotional landscape. Furthermore, I obtained certification in youth mental health first aid, equipping myself to support struggling youth. Currently, I'm pursuing certification in QPR (Question, Persuade, Refer). It is another valuable method used to intervene effectively in suicidal ideation.

Fueled by a belief in the power of QPR training, I see it as a crucial weapon in the fight against suicide. QPR equips people to recognize the warning signs of crisis, intervene effectively, and ultimately save lives. The reality is that these signs are often hidden in plain sight, but we often miss them. By educating ourselves, we can become a safety net for those struggling in silence. My ultimate goal is to work with at-risk youth, helping them understand that a bad day is simply a temporary setback. It is not the end of the journey. Though it might seem scary, the dark night will pass eventually. We can work through challenges together, and there is always hope.

This passion for youth mental health also led me to collaborate with the school board. Together, we implemented a new program called Hope Squad in our local middle school. Hope Squad is an evidence-based program that harnesses the power of peer connection to prevent suicide. This program is particularly relevant for our middle school, which serves grades 6-8 and acts as a point of integration for students from three different elementary schools.

At this crucial developmental stage, adolescents are navigating complex social dynamics and a heightened sense of self-awareness. Hope Squad provides a framework for building a strong support system during this critical time. Trained student members can identify peers who might be struggling, fostering a sense of belonging and offering a safe space to confide. This peer-to-peer approach can be incredibly effective in reaching at-risk youth who might be hesitant to seek help from adults.

As someone who has traversed the depths of emotional pain, I've come to understand the vital role of support systems and resilience in navigating life's challenges. Just as I've discovered the power of embracing sorrow as part of our journey, so too have I witnessed the transformative impact of strong support networks. In our most vulnerable moments, it's often the hands extended by others that guide us toward light and hope.

Throughout my healing journey, I've learned that healing isn't about erasing the pain. To assuage the suffering of emotional pain, we can't pop an Advil or two. The process of healing is about interlacing the sorrow into our existence, allowing it to coexist with the love and joy that life still offers. My experience has been a profound teacher, revealing that even in the depths of despair, the potential for strength and growth lies dormant. It's a resilience that emerges from the ashes, and this willpower is a beautiful reflection of an enduring human spirit.

The pain of losing AJ will forever be a part of me. It will be a constant echo in the chambers of my hollow heart. It occupies the space where AJ once existed. However, it no longer dictates the course of my life. I stand before you as a reflection of the unyielding spirit – as a reminder that we have the ability to rise above tragedy. Even in the face of unimaginable loss, when life loses all meaning, we can find purpose. Along my journey, I have witnessed the transformative power of grief – a power that can forge strength from suffering and purpose from pain.

Instead of reliving the shadows of my loss, I share my story to kindle a flicker of hope within you. We all navigate our own turbulent journeys. This is why I pray for each one of us who has suffered the tremendous loss of a loved one, who is enduring their demons in silence, and who has given up in life. May we find the fortitude to conquer these challenges, transforming the raw wounds of pain into an unyielding source of strength. Let us not succumb to the suffocating silence surrounding mental health but become champions of open dialogue. It's in the face of immense hardship that the human spirit unveils its extraordinary resilience, blossoming like a tenacious wildflower pushing through concrete.

CHAPTER SIX

The Struggle for Normalcy

How do you describe a sense of normalcy? It used to be the smell of coffee brewing as I woke up, the happy chaos of getting AJ ready for school, and the echo of his laughter bouncing off the walls after he'd pull a prank. Normal meant chiding him; it meant watching from the sidelines with a mixture of awe and horror as he'd pull off something just because he was dared. Now, it feels like a foreign language, a memory from a past life I can't quite piece together.

Losing AJ shattered my world. It's like trying to put together a puzzle with missing pieces. Only these missing pieces come together to construct who I used to be when everything was 'normal.' Now, every morning is a battle, and dragging myself out of bed feels like pushing through quicksand. There are days when his absence leaves me gasping for air. The suffocating grief is a relentless current that pulls me under with the weight of his loss. My heart feels like a shattered mirror, reflecting a distorted version of myself. How can life be normal when a third of your heart is just gone?

Invisible suffering allows you to mask your pain with practiced smiles, keeping your struggles a private affair. But grieving in the public eye, like at funerals, creates a different kind of burden. While the initial wave of support is comforting, there's a strange pressure that sets in later. It feels as though there's an unspoken expectation to heal on someone else's timeline. The implication becomes you owe it to those who supported you to get better, almost as if their efforts will be deemed wasted if you don't bounce back according to their timetable.

There's this constant pressure - this expectation to just get over it - to put on a brave face and pretend everything's okay. But how can I when the simplest tasks feel like climbing Mount Everest? Each breath is a conscious effort, a fight against the tide of grief that threatens to consume me. I miss him in the quiet moments, the noisy moments, every single moment. There's no normalcy here, just the raw, brutal ache of a love forever unfinished.

I absolutely wouldn't want to come across as ungrateful. In these depths of despair, the support of loved ones is a lifeline. They try, they truly do. Their condolences, their gentle words of sympathy – I see the effort, the love behind them. But there's a disconnect, a one-sidedness to it all. It's like they're speaking a different dialect of grief, one that can't quite capture the hollowness that reverberates within me. How could they possibly understand the sheer magnitude of this pain, the suffocating absence that echoes in every corner of my being?

Despite the struggle, I put on a brave face for my other children. I go through the motions, this daily charade of normalcy, but the exhaustion is relentless. Parenting through this suffocating grief feels like navigating a maze blindfolded. Each step I take is tentative, and each decision feels fraught with the fear of making a colossal mistake.

Some mornings, I wake up with a jolt, feeling a desperate hope clinging to me like a life raft. Maybe it was all a horrible dream - a cruel trick my mind played, I repeatedly tell myself. I keep my eyes shut, already feeling the tears welling in them, but I stay in denial. Then reality slams into me like a rogue wave, stealing the breath from my lungs. It's Groundhog Day from hell, this forced replay of the nightmare that has become my life. There's no escape - only the agonizing replay of the news, the phone calls, the crushing weight of confirmation.

Functioning with a heart fractured into a million shards is an ordeal in itself. Each day feels like a marathon I never signed up for, my body a leaden weight dragging against the current. Every step sends a fresh wave of pain pulsating through me, constantly reminding me of the gaping hole in my soul. Dates and times blur together. With AJ gone, they're meaningless markers in a reality that's lost all definition. Time itself seems to have taken a detour, swallowed whole by the abyss my son's absence has carved out.

My other children, my precious boys with their wide, innocent eyes, are grappling with their own storm of emotions. How do I explain the inexplicable and make them understand the seismic shift that has shattered not just our family but my very core? I want to scream, to let loose the torrent of grief that threatens to drown me, but their fragile faces hold me back. I need to be strong for them, the one constant in a world that's come unmoored. How can I shield them from the raw edges of my grief, the bottomless well of despair that threatens to swallow me whole? At the same time, how can I be honest about the pain that consumes every waking moment? I need them to know, with every fiber of my depleted being, that I'm still here for them. They are my anchors through this storm.

The isolation cuts deep. It's like being stranded on a deserted island, surrounded by people on the mainland who can't quite reach me. Their gazes flicker with a mix of pity and awkwardness, then dart away. Maybe they don't know what words to offer, or perhaps they wonder if I did something wrong or if this tragedy is somehow my fault. The truth is, their averted eyes don't lessen the crushing weight of grief that chains me down. Every day feels like being pummeled by a rough wave of emotions - a tsunami of despair, anger, and a hollowness that aches to the very core.

Grief is a paradox. Sometimes, it's a feral scream trapped in my throat, a primal urge to shout my pain to the heavens until the world hears. It claws at me, demanding to be acknowledged, to be seen in its raw, devastating form. But then, the tide recedes, leaving behind a hollow ache that craves quietude. I pull on a mask of forced normalcy, a thin smile to shield those around me from the wreckage within.

Talking about AJ isn't a plea for pity. It's a necessity, a way to keep him tethered to this world. He existed vibrantly, undeniably. He mattered, not for the way his story ended, but for the beautiful young man he was, the light he brought into my life. So when I speak of him, don't turn away. Don't pretend he was a ghost, a tragedy to be whispered about and forgotten. Listen. Listen to his story, the impact he had on me, on us. Because even though he's gone, his memory lives on. It lives in every tear that escapes my eyes, in every ragged beat of my shattered heart. And that, my friend, is a story worth remembering.

Is it possible to be a good mom anymore? That's the question that taunts me every single day. It's a constant battle raging inside me - a tug-of-war between the fierce love I have for my boys and this all-consuming fear. I just want to give them the world - everything they could ever dream of, but then this terror grips me, this urge to wrap them in bubble wrap and never let them go.

There's this overwhelming sense of guilt that hangs over me like a dark cloud, whispering cruel reminders of all the things I never got to do for AJ. Every time I see my other boys' faces light up with excitement over something as simple as a new toy or a trip to the park, it's like a knife to the heart. How can I deny them anything when all I crave is to have AJ back, to give him all those experiences he'll never have? It's just not fair.

But then there's the fear. It's a paralyzing thing, this fear. Icy claws grip me every time I let them out of my sight. What if something happens to them too? What if the world snatches them away just like it took AJ? The thought of losing another piece of my heart, of it shattering into dust, is a constant struggle, this balancing act between love and fear, between wanting to give them the world and wanting to protect them from it. But amidst all the chaos and uncertainty, there's one thing I know for sure: I will love them fiercely, with every fiber of my being, for as long as I have breath in my body.

In the depths of my shattered heart, I find the strength to rise above the pain of losing AJ. It is a pain that may never fully heal, but I refuse to let it consume me. Instead, I am determined to become the best damn parent I can be, not in spite of my grief but because of it. AJ's untimely departure has taught me a profound lesson - that life is a fragile gift, fleeting and precious. It reminds me to cherish every moment with the ones I love, never taking their presence for granted.

I refuse to allow the grief of losing AJ to control me, even if it may have broken my heart, and my heart may never heal completely. I promise to be the best darn parent I can be - not despite, but precisely because of my loss. If there's one thing that AJ's passing has taught me, it's that life is short and valuable and that we should cherish every second we spend with the people we love. Alternatively, it could be that I'm afraid to open myself to them and show them the unvarnished, untidy truth of my sadness. Even though I feel like I'm drowning in misery, I smile, nod, and act like everything is fine. I don't want to weigh them down with my suffering or lower their emotions with my tears.

However, there are other times when loneliness seems like a physical pain, an emptiness in my stomach that cannot be filled with any amount of love or support. Those are the times when I most yearn for connection, when I want to be seen, heard and understood.

Thus, I tentatively extend my hand to see if anyone is up for plunging beside me into the depths of my hopelessness. And occasionally, miraculously, someone reaches back in a show of support and empathy. And for a brief while, if not longer, the loneliness disappears in such moments. Because it helps to know that I'm not alone in my suffering, even though my grief may never completely go away.

CHAPTER SEVEN

Finding Healing Through Counseling

Grief is a universal experience, but the ways we navigate it are as unique as the people we are. Some find solace in throwing themselves into work, while others seek comfort in quiet reflection. And there are some who seek solace in the most advised method of healing – therapy. There's a strange resistance to the idea of therapy, a sort of aversion to the thought of peeling back the layers of our pain in front of a complete stranger. It can feel baffling, this idea of being vulnerable to someone you just met. But trust me, after much deliberation and a leap of faith, I can say this: therapy does help. It's a space where you can shed the masks you wear for the world, a place where the tangled mess of emotions can begin to unravel. My journey of healing was marked by these roller-coasters of emotions as well.

As I reflect on the moment I first considered seeking counseling, I felt incredibly apprehensive. It was beyond my understanding how someone could unveil their deepest hurts before a stranger.

The idea of spilling my guts, all the joys and sorrows, the tangled mess of my life, to a complete stranger - it felt like jumping into a bottomless pit, blindfolded. I was reluctant to dive into the depths of everything that had happened to me. How could I bring myself to confront the raw truths I had been holding inside? Could I even peel back the layers and expose the raw, vulnerable core beneath? Could I trust this person with the avalanche of fears and hurts I carried like a lead weight in my chest?

These questions swirled in my mind, casting doubt on the notion of seeking help. It took an immense amount of internal dialogue before I finally took the leap into counseling. The initial sessions were a blur of tentative words and choked-back tears. It wasn't easy. But with each session, a tiny shift occurred. The moment I started opening up, a sense of relief washed over me. The burden of carrying my emotions alone began to lift, and I found solace in the act of sharing my struggles with a compassionate listener. In that vulnerable space, I discovered the strength to confront my inner turmoil, and for the first time, I felt the warmth of hope seep into my soul. The journey was daunting, but the decision to seek counseling became a pivotal turning point in my life.

Before counseling, words were like tangled knots in my stomach. I yearned to express what churned inside - the good, the bad, the confusing mess of emotions, but they just wouldn't come out. How could I express myself when I couldn’t voice my inner turmoil? My counselor had a way of gently coaxing those knots loose. It felt like an excavation as we unearthed buried feelings layer by layer. Some were raw and painful, while others were surprisingly complex, but I learned to understand them and accept them.

With each truth came a cataclysmic release - a sigh of relief that I hadn't even realized I was holding. We untangled the web of emotions tied to my loss, including the ones I'd tried to bury deep down. We explored not just the recent ones but things that stretched back to childhood, hidden away by denial and a desperate hope they'd just disappear. AJ's spirit helped me confront those painful truths, not with judgment, but with understanding. It was a long journey, but slowly, I began to understand myself better - why I felt the way I did and where these emotions stemmed from. It wasn't just about processing the loss; it was about processing a lifetime of unspoken feelings. And that, in itself, was a form of healing.

The pain of losing my child was a gaping wound. It felt compounded by the stigma surrounding his death, making it an intensely personal tragedy I couldn't share freely. Even talking about it was excruciating. Whenever I'd try to open up, the words were choked by a torrent of tears that threatened to drown any semblance of coherence. The world felt deafeningly silent, a place where my grief seemed to resonate only within the cavernous emptiness of my own being.

In that suffocating darkness, counseling became a guiding light. It offered an unbiased human connection - a safe harbor from the judgmental storms swirling outside. Here, I could speak to someone who knew nothing about our story. Therapy provided me with a blank slate upon which I could paint the raw canvas of my grief. This therapist wasn't a friend or family member burdened by the weight of shared history or the constraints of social niceties. She could offer professional objectivity and a steady hand guiding me through the treacherous emotional terrain.

As a sense of trust blossomed, the dam within me began to crack. I hesitantly started to share my deepest fears and insecurities, the ones I couldn't voice for fear of judgment or misunderstanding. There was a profound comfort in knowing she wasn't there to judge but to understand. The world felt isolating at times. It was a place where the immensity of my trauma seemed to render me an alien. But with her, there was a shared language of empathy, even if she couldn't fully grasp the specific nuances of my emotions. She understood the profound impact of my trauma, the invisible scars etched deep by my loss. It was a bridge across the chasm of grief built on the solid ground of professional expertise and genuine human connection.

Throughout my counseling journey, I predominantly engaged in individual therapy, never venturing into the realm of group sessions. However, there was one occasion when I attended a session with Gavin. Although the focus was on his progression and how he coped with his own struggles, that session unexpectedly became a pivotal moment for me. His perspective and experiences forced me to introspect upon my own feelings of shame.

The loss had shattered my very core. The foundation of my identity as a mother crumbled, replaced by a suffocating self-doubt. Every memory, every action, and every interaction was scrutinized through the distorting lens of grief. Did I miss a sign? Could I have done more? These questions became a relentless internal monologue, fueling my crippling sense of inadequacy.

My therapist played a significant role in helping me navigate these feelings. She encouraged me to ask myself tough questions: "What makes you think this is your fault? Why do you believe you missed something?" With gentle guidance, she encouraged me to dissect these thoughts, to examine the root of this self-blame. Sometimes, the simple act of verbalizing these anxieties, having them reflected back through a neutral lens, was a form of therapy in itself.

It was a revelation. Throughout my life, I'd held the belief that true comfort came from someone who knew our entire story and could offer feedback steeped in the context of our lives. But this unbiased perspective, this outsider's view, proved to be profoundly transformative. It jolted me out of the suffocating echo chamber of my grief, allowing me to see things with a newfound clarity. It wasn't about having someone know every detail but about having someone who could guide me toward self-compassion and understanding. This unbiased perspective, stripped of the emotional weight of the situation, allowed me to confront these anxieties head-on. I was able to dismantle the scaffolding of self-blame I'd constructed. It was a long and arduous journey, but with each session, a sliver of self-doubt chipped away, replaced by a fragile sense of self-acceptance.

Yet, there were days when the grief felt like a tidal wave, threatening to pull me under. On those days, my therapist became my anchor, giving me tools to help me weather the storm. These weren't just techniques for our sessions; they were coping mechanisms for the in-between. They helped me during the days when I wouldn't see her and the moments when the pain felt particularly raw.

One strategy that resonated deeply was the concept of an emotional storage unit. She suggested that when a wave of emotion hit me at an inconvenient time, like a trigger at work, I shouldn't feel pressured to deal with it right then. Instead, I could visualize a safe haven, a little barn with a sliding door. Here, I could store those overwhelming feelings for later, a place where I could process them without the chaos of daily life swirling around me. Using imagination was a powerful way to acknowledge my emotions without letting them consume me entirely.

Another crucial aspect of healing she emphasized was mindfulness. In the throes of grief, it's easy to lose yourself in the whirlwind. She encouraged me to take those moments of intense sadness and focus on small techniques to ground myself. Deep breaths and progressive muscle relaxation – these simple practices pulled me back from the emotional abyss. This focus on self-care was a significant transformation in my life. As a mom and a nurse, taking care of myself has always been an afterthought. I instinctively put everyone else's needs before my own. It was a habit that had only exacerbated the pain, and I hadn't even realized that. My therapist gently nudged me toward establishing healthy routines and prioritizing sleep and healthy meals. She emphasized how physical activity could be a way to channel pent-up emotions for me. We even explored Emotional Freedom Techniques (tapping), a practice that offered a surprising blend of relaxation and focus shift. It wasn't a distraction but a way to gently ease my racing thoughts and bring a sense of calm.

Through it all, her unwavering support was a constant source of strength. When the world felt overwhelming, she'd remind me, "Okay, Crystal, let's take a deep breath. We're going to slow things down. We'll get through this, one step at a time." These tools, these coping mechanisms, allowed me to not just survive the crushing weight of grief but to slowly, ever so slowly, begin to rebuild.

Before learning these techniques, I was a chronic multitasker, juggling a hundred things at once. My therapist helped me see the cracks in that strategy; it wasn't healthy. We explored ways to channel my grief into something positive. I took up the hobby of scrapbooking, a way to preserve memories and create a tangible tribute to my child. Moreover, creating some sort of memorial routine added a sense of stability to my life.

Another crucial skill I learned was setting boundaries. This applied even to family members. Sometimes, a simple "no" was all it took to shield my emotions from getting overwhelmed. It felt like I was building a fence around myself. It felt like my therapist was giving me a toolbox filled with coping mechanisms. Deep breaths, mindfulness exercises, even tapping – these techniques became my crutches during emotional crises. Through it all, I started to feel a sense of renewal. I had always been the helper - the one taking care of others. But counseling taught me to prioritize self-care.

For so long, I'd focused on helping others, neglecting my own needs. Counseling taught me that self-care wasn't selfish; it was essential. As strange as it sounds, I began to see grief not as something to overcome but as a way to stay connected to my loved ones.

Growing up, I never talked about my feelings. I was what you might call a "bottler." Everything went in, shoved down deep. Even the smallest thing could set me off because I had so many pent-up emotions. Counseling helped me crack open that bottle. Now, I'm slowly learning to identify my emotions to actually talk about them. It's a struggle; some days are even harder than others, but I'm getting better. For that, I'll be forever grateful to my therapist because grief shattered my identity. It made me question everything: who I was as a nurse, a mom, a wife. My purpose in life felt like a wisp of smoke, swirling and disappearing. However, I'm slowly incorporating the loss into the narrative of who I am. It's a painful process, but it's allowing me to embrace the present. It teaches me to be truly present in the here and now without dwelling on the past or fearing the future. It helps me savor the joy that still exists and emerge from this grief as a changed person - not the same, but stronger, more resilient, overflowing with compassion and a newfound authenticity.

In my ongoing journey through life, the challenges remain frequent, but navigating them is gradually becoming a bit easier. At first, I was very hesitant to show my emotions to others due to fear of judgment and shame. Now, I realize how misguided that was. My counselor helped me understand that it's okay to cry to feel angry or sad whenever and however I need to. Before, I would suppress these feelings, telling myself, "No, Crystal. You can't do this." Along my journey of healing, I've realized how unhealthy that was.

Every day, I'm getting better at handling my emotions. My counselor encouraged me to surround myself with friends and family who understand and can provide comfort instead of isolating myself. When I'm having a bad day or struggling, I've learned to reach out sooner rather than later. Talking things out with someone often helps more than crying alone. She also taught me about setting realistic expectations for my grieving process. There's no right or wrong way to grieve, and it's not a linear path. She taught me to be gentle with myself and to allow breaks when needed. Sometimes, just stepping outside to get some fresh air and sunlight can work wonders. There's something almost magical about the sunlight and fresh air; they help me reset and work through the emotions I'm experiencing at the moment. Thanks to her guidance, I'm learning to embrace my feelings and seek support when I need it. This journey is still tough, but I'm finding ways to cope and gradually heal.

With each therapy session, it felt as though the intricate knots of grief surrounding me began to untangle, unraveling gradually. In the midst of the shadows, I began to discern faint glimmers of light, rediscovering latent strengths and dormant passions. I learned to pay homage to my child's memory not solely through tears but with heartfelt remembrance and profound gratitude. Throughout his life, he was so radiant that he motivated me to shine brightly in his honor.

Above all, I am cultivating patience and self-compassion. It's an ongoing journey, and while I am far from perfect, I sense a gradual easing with time. Initially, grief felt like an intense battlefield, and each step was fraught with uncertainty. However, through therapy and the support of loved ones, it began to morph into less of a battleground and more of an unexplored terrain. I found myself pondering, how do I navigate this unfamiliar landscape? It was akin to the phoenix's legendary rebirth from ashes; despite my soul's fragmentation from loss, I endeavor daily to lift myself from the wreckage of four years past.

Sometimes, I contemplate the idea of returning to therapy, sensing it could offer ongoing support and guidance. Perhaps one day, I'll revisit that path. But for now, I feel empowered with the strength and compassion to navigate each day, propelled by the desire to honor AJ's memory. I've undergone a profound transformation, allowing myself to reclaim my humanity and relinquish the burden of unrealistic expectations. It's a departure from how I used to perceive imperfections, now embracing them as integral facets of life.

Make no mistake; therapy doesn't numb. It doesn't make you randomly a happy person, either. It's not a cure. On the contrary, it gives us strategies to deal with the pain. Whenever I think about AJ's smile, I feel my chest clench tightly. I believe there's no force in the world that can heal my aching heart. AJ's absence has left a void that nothing else can fill - a palpable emptiness where grief takes root. Yet, I'm slowly untangling those roots, learning to embrace love and life once more. Despite the ache of his birthdays, we've established a new tradition within our family. Instead of dwelling on what should have been, we gather to send Chinese lanterns adorned with heartfelt messages into the night sky, a luminous tribute to the son we hold dear in our hearts.

Like me, there are many others who are trying to recover from this horrible suffering, and I hope to stand by them. For the longest time, it seemed like support groups for moms who had lost children were scarce. But recently, I discovered a group of mothers who, like me, had experienced this profound loss. Bonding with them and sharing our grief with those who truly understand has been an incredibly transformative part of my healing journey. In addition to this newfound connection, I attended a grieving mom's retreat not long ago. Surrounded by about 15 other mothers who had endured similar tragedies, we spent four days together, sharing our stories and granting ourselves grace. Being in the company of others who have walked this painful path made a world of difference.

When I arrived at the retreat, my heart felt heavy with grief. But as I left just a few days later, I noticed a slight lightening of that burden. The experience introduced me to new ways of nurturing myself and fostering my healing process. For this, I am endlessly grateful. The support and understanding I found in these fellow grieving mothers have been invaluable in my journey toward healing and finding solace.

Throughout my journey, I've learned that healing isn't a sudden sunrise after a long night; it's a gradual coaxing of light from the horizon. There will be days so heavy it feels like the world itself is pressing down on you, days when the mere act of breathing seems like a herculean effort. But somewhere along the line, almost imperceptibly, the crushing weight begins to ease. You might wake up one morning and realize the death wish that had been a constant companion has vanished, replaced by a faint flicker of hope. It's a fragile thing, this newfound appreciation, but with each sunrise, it strengthens. You start noticing the small things – the warmth of the sun on your skin, the sound of laughter, the love in the eyes of a loved one. It's a slow process, this journey of healing, but with each step, the path ahead seems a little less daunting and the possibility of joy a little more real.

CHAPTER EIGHT
The Journey of Self-Discovery

Our personality begins to take shape in childhood. By the age of 25, it is said that our minds are fully formed. As young adults, we often believe we have charted our course in life – we have laid down the roots of our careers, and many of us have chosen our life partners. In our self-assurance, we convince ourselves that we have reached maturity, but this is rarely true. Age is just a number, and I believe we continue to evolve throughout our lives. This harsh truth becomes evident when we lose someone we love more than anything. When we take a plunge into the gloomy depths of grief, we unveil the complexities of human character. It turns our world upside-down and shifts our entire perspective on life. For me, this realization hit me after I lost AJ. The person I was before could never have navigated the depths of despair and emerged to see the world as I do now. I'm not merely searching for a silver lining in my suffering; rather, this growth and self-discovery are the natural outcomes of tragedy.

Looking back, I acknowledge that going through that grief was brutal, but it forced me to figure out who I was again. It wasn't easy; the whole journey was like walking a maze blindfolded. There were breakdowns and dark days, but also these little glimmers of hope that kept me going. The more I dealt with everything, the clearer things became. Every challenge made me tougher. Now, I have a better idea of what I want in life, and I'm starting to feel that happiness again. It's like rediscovering all the good stuff life has to offer.

This adversity has etched new dimensions into my character and outlook on life. When I lost AJ, it felt as if the world changed instantly. His death was shadowed by stigma and mental health struggles. It inflicted a pain on me and our family that was deeply personal and profoundly isolating. The routines and roles that once defined me, especially my role as a nurse, suddenly lost their significance. Previously, being a nurse had always been a core part of my identity. However, after losing AJ, it felt empty and meaningless. Will I continue as a nurse? I often find myself wondering, but I still don't know the answer to that. I am still going through the motions and still maintaining my responsibilities, but they no longer hold the same purpose for me. Where this journey will take me remains uncertain.

This profound encounter has not only disrupted the delicate balance of my social interactions but also affected my family life. Now, mothering has become an uphill battle for me, fraught with loss and detachment. I increasingly lean on my immediate family and a select few close friends to maintain my sanity. Their support has become my lifeline, offering the stability and strength necessary to get through each day in this altered reality. My journey of rediscovery began with cautious steps as I delved into understanding mental health, not just as a coping mechanism for my loss but also as a tribute to AJ's memory. It's a perplexing yet captivating process. Exploring the depths of my anguish has unveiled a new purpose: advocacy for mental health awareness and support for those facing similar struggles. Embracing this mission allows me to transform my grief into meaningful action, rebuilding a sense of self with this newfound purpose.

In the aftermath of AJ's passing, I found myself confronted with intense and unfiltered emotions. I had to navigate through the rawness of grief to seek not only answers but also to embrace the vulnerability inherent in facing tragedy head-on. Living with this open narrative demanded authenticity - a willingness to bear my soul and share my truth. Therefore, opening up about my pain and struggles became an integral part of my healing journey. Being vulnerable fostered connections with others who had experienced similar losses. The network of support and understanding that emerged from these newfound connections has been nothing short of remarkable.

Now, authenticity has become a guiding principle in this new chapter of my life. By sharing my true self and embracing vulnerability, I've discovered a sense of community and understanding that transcends words. Although this journey toward self-compassion and healing is challenging, it has been immensely rewarding. Despite the temptation to wear a mask and project strength, I've found solace in being authentically myself. This honesty has allowed me to pass through the twists and turns of this unfamiliar path with courage.

One thing I've gleaned from this experience is that resilience isn't a one-click restart button. It isn't necessarily about bouncing back to a previous state, but it includes integrating the loss into a new way of being. The ache lingers like a phantom limb - a constant echo of what used to be. But from the cracks, something unexpected sprouts – a strength I never knew I possessed - a transformation forged in the fiery furnace of grief. Just as a crumpled piece of paper cannot revert to its original uncreased form, the experience of sorrow leaves lasting marks that persist. Anyone who suggests otherwise may not fully comprehend the depth of what you are undergoing. However, it is important to remember that with each passing day, the situation gradually improves, and healing becomes possible.

Every small step forward felt like a personal triumph. It felt like defiance against the overwhelming tide of sadness weighing me down. It reignited a long-dormant purpose within me. The idea of a non-profit organization, which was initially a flickering candle in the dark, blossomed into something much bigger. It became a platform to offer the very comfort I once desperately craved. In the aftermath of my loss, spreading mental health awareness became my new mission. Through outreach programs and educational initiatives, I chip away at the stigma, a stubborn wall that isolates and silences. It's a monumental task – dismantling a mountain of misunderstanding, but I find solace in this challenge. It is an attempt to pay tribute to my AJ's memory. It exemplifies the resilient human spirit, which can not only endure but thrive in the face of unthinkable loss.

It's both comforting and bittersweet to find that even in the midst of deep pain, there's hope and support waiting on the other side. Coming to terms with the fact that life is fleeting has taught me to cherish every moment to really be present in the here and now. I've learned to see beauty in the little moments that come and go, which has given me a greater sense of gratitude for the meaningful connections in my life. Going through grief has taught me to give myself the space to feel and heal. Realizing the strength and resilience I have within, especially in tough times, has given me a newfound sense of purpose and optimism for the future. Though I sometimes wish I could turn back the hands of time, spend one more moment with AJ, hear him out, and save him somehow, I also feel hopeful about what lies ahead. This journey of self-discovery hasn't been easy, but it's been incredibly transformative. Despite the ups and downs, I'm starting to see the potential for growth and positive change, and that gives me hope for what's to come.

In the process of reclaiming joy, my husband and I have found our own limits, insecurities, and individuality. Every day feels like a precious gift now. It's a grim yet inspiring reminder that tomorrow isn't a promise, and that's sharpened my focus on the simple joys life offers. It's the kind of joy I find tucked away in everyday moments, like watching the goofy grins spread across Gavin and Keegan's faces. They're here, with me, healthy and happy, and that's all that truly matters. I savor every second I get with them, trying to be truly present to soak it all in.

However, life has become about more than just cherishing these precious moments with my boys. Sharing my story, advocating for mental health awareness, and educating others – that's become a real wellspring of purpose for me. It gives my days a new kind of meaning. It gives me a reason to get out of bed in the morning with a fire in my belly.

Of course, writing about such a personal experience is completely new territory as well. It's raw, and it makes me vulnerable in a way I never expected. There is something about written words that amplifies the ephemeral nature of those fleeting experiences, making them more evocative. It bestows upon the past an intensified sense of haunting as if the memories become even more real when captured in written form. However, these words have also opened doors to this incredible sense of community. I'm meeting amazing people who've been touched by my story and people who are walking similar paths. It's a connection I never thought I'd find, and it's a reflection of the power of vulnerability. By opening myself up, I've found a whole new way to connect with the world, and that's a beautiful thing.

The journey through grief has definitely woven a tighter web of connection between me and the people around me. Every conversation feels more profound, with a shared understanding simmering just beneath the surface. It's like we've all peeked behind the curtain, glimpsed the raw vulnerability of life, and emerged with a newfound appreciation for the simple act of being there for each other. These connections are the threads that are slowly but surely stitching my life back together, painting a canvas richer and more meaningful than before. My newfound purpose extends beyond just the connections I've fostered. It's not just about seeking support but also returning to the world. It compels me to reach out to others who are facing similar darkness. Having walked that harrowing path myself, as a parent who's lost a child, I feel a responsibility to offer what solace I can.

So, here's what I want to say to anyone grappling with this unimaginable loss: allow yourself to grieve. It's not a weakness. It's a necessity. Feel every jagged emotion that claws its way to the surface – the gut-wrenching sadness, the white-hot anger, the paralyzing confusion. Don't let anyone tell you to suppress it or to put on a brave face. Grieve fiercely, grieve deeply, because in the crucible of your pain lies the potential for healing. There will be days when it feels like you're drowning in sorrow, days when the thought of moving on seems like a betrayal. But know this: you are not alone in this storm. There are hands reaching out to help you weather it, and on the other side, you'll find a strength you never knew you possessed. It's a long and winding road, but with each step you take, the path ahead will begin to illuminate, leading you toward a future where the memory of your child lives on, cherished, and woven into the fabric of your being.

The biggest regret I have looking back is all that time I spent trying to be stoic. Stuffing down my grief and pretending everything was okay only prolonged the pain. What I've come to understand is that creating space for your feelings is absolutely essential. Let the wave of grief wash over you, even if it happens every day. Every single emotion deserves to be acknowledged without judgment. Don't try to edit yourself; don't try to minimize your pain.

For me, tears were a release valve, a way to let some of the pressure escape. But grief is a personal journey, and everyone finds their own way to heal. There's no one-size-fits-all. Maybe writing becomes your sanctuary it's a way to translate the storm within you onto paper. Perhaps art becomes your voice, a canvas to express the emotions you can't quite find the words for. Or maybe movement is your medicine, a way to process the heavyweight in your body, one step or stride at a time. There's no right or wrong way to grieve. Just allow yourself to feel whatever that means for you.

This grief will come in waves like the tide surging and receding. There will be days when the sun peeks through the clouds, offering a glimpse of hope. And there will be days where you feel like you're being dragged under by the current. But through it all, remember to be your own biggest advocate. Be patient with yourself. Don't be afraid to ask for help – it's a sign of strength, not weakness. Reach out to your loved ones, and lean on your friends and family. Explore therapy or join a support group – these can be lifelines of comfort and understanding. You are worthy of love and support, and there are people who want to walk beside you on this difficult path.

Grief can sap your energy, making even the simplest tasks feel monumental. Brushing your teeth, showering, changing clothes – all these things that used to be routine can become overwhelming hurdles. It's easy to fall into a pattern of withdrawal, wanting nothing more than to curl up in bed and shut the world out. Believe me, I've been there. Self-care can feel impossible during this time, but it's crucial. Just like a car needs fuel to run, your body needs nourishment and rest to weather this emotional storm. Prioritize getting enough sleep, even if it's just short stretches at first. Eat healthy meals, even if it means starting with small, manageable portions. Force yourself to take a walk outside – nature has a remarkable way of calming the soul. Don't underestimate the power of movement; even a gentle stroll can work wonders for your mood and energy levels. Taking care of your emotional well-being is equally important. Bottling up emotions can only lead to long-term distress.

In the thick of grief, it's easy to let your emotional reserves dwindle to dust. You become this raw nerve, perpetually exposed, and the idea of one more thing, one more person, can feel unbearable. That's when I learned the power of boundaries. It wasn't about being cold or shutting people out but about creating a safe space for myself to heal. Saying no to extra commitments and politely declining social gatherings when I was running on fumes. Others might accuse you of being anti-social, but by creating boundaries, you're only trying to preserve your energy.

However, grief, as heavy and all-encompassing as it can be, doesn't extinguish your spirit entirely. There's still a flicker of light waiting to be rekindled. For me, that meant rediscovering activities that nourished my soul. Maybe it was getting lost in a new hobby. For another parent, it might be something like learning to bake sourdough bread. For me, it meant simply stepping outside, feeling the sun on my face, and reacquainting myself with the beauty of nature. Even a small dose of something that uplifted my spirit, even for a fleeting moment, made a world of difference. Grief is a winding path with no map and no clear destination. Acknowledge that you understand that it is a natural process and there is no definitive right or wrong way to go through it. However, remember to extend the same compassion to yourself that you would offer to others or to a friend in a similar situation. It is important to set realistic expectations for yourself as you navigate this process.

Losing a child to the dark claws of mental illness is a monstrous thing - a loss that defies all logic and understanding. It leaves you searching for meaning in the face of something so senseless. For me, solace arrived in the form of purpose. Honoring Aidan's memory became my guiding light. The Aidan J. Foster Memorial Scholarship, a beacon in his name, allowed us to channel our grief into something positive. It became a way to create a legacy, a ripple of kindness that would extend far beyond our personal pain. But it wasn't just about Aidan. We saw a chance to make a difference on a larger scale. It was a way to turn our pain into purpose, to find meaning in the midst of grief. I encourage other suffering parents to do the same.

There are still dark days, moments when the weight of loss threatens to drown me. But in those moments, I cling to a sliver of hope, a belief that with time and support, the path ahead will reveal slivers of light and healing. Remember, you are not alone. Even in the deepest valleys of grief, there are people who care and want to walk beside you on this difficult journey. Find those people, hold onto them, and know that even in the darkest night, the stars are still there, waiting to shine through the clouds.

Made in the USA
Middletown, DE
09 July 2024